Now Is the Time

NOW IS THE TIME

The Urgent Call to Repent and Follow Jesus

BY

Mitch Howell

RESOURCE *Publications* · Eugene, Oregon

NOW IS THE TIME
The Urgent Call to Repent and Follow Jesus

Resource Publications
An Imprint of Wipf and Stock Publishers
199 W. 8th Ave., Suite 3
Eugene, OR 97401

www.wipfandstock.com

PAPERBACK ISBN: 979-8-3852-6246-5
HARDCOVER ISBN: 979-8-3852-6247-2
EBOOK ISBN: 979-8-3852-6248-9

VERSION NUMBER 10/06/25

Preface

The world is asleep at the wheel. The church is nodding off in the passenger seat, lulled by comforts, politics, entertainment, and half-truths. But the trumpet is about to sound. Time is short. And now is not the moment to hit snooze; now is the time to wake up, rise up, and repent.

This book is not for the lukewarm. It is not for those satisfied with a Sunday-only faith or a convenient Jesus. It is for those who sense the shaking. Those who feel the urgency. Who know deep in their bones that things are not as they seem, and that judgment begins in the house of God.

We are not waiting on the last days; we are living in them. The hour is late. And while the world plunges into darkness, the true church must burn brighter than ever, not with noise or spectacle, but with holiness, obedience, and boldness.

If you are tired of powerless religion, of empty words, of compromise wrapped in Christianese, then this is your wake-up call, not from me, but from the Spirit of God. He is calling his people back to himself. He is preparing a bride without spot or wrinkle. And he is separating the wheat from the tares.

There is no more time to waste. No more playing it safe. No more straddling the fence. Jesus is coming soon. And he's not returning for a crowd; he's returning for a remnant. Those who know him, follow him, and are unashamed to live and die for him.

Now is the time to repent. Now is the time to believe. Now is the time to follow Jesus with everything you have.

This message is urgent because eternity is real. Heaven is real. Hell is real. And souls are hanging in the balance.

May this book stir your soul, convict your heart, and draw you into deeper surrender. And may the Spirit of the living God fall afresh on every person who turns these pages, in Jesus' name. Amen.

Opening Prayer

Heavenly Father, I come before you with trembling and gratitude. You are holy, righteous, and full of mercy. Thank you for the gift of salvation through your Son, Jesus Christ. Thank you for loving us while we were still sinners.

Lord, I pray that this book would not be just another book, but a vessel. A tool. A holy warning. A call to come out from among the world and be separate. May it reach the lost, convict the wandering, and strengthen the faithful.

Let every word be soaked in your Spirit. Let every chapter echo what you are saying in this hour. Speak through these pages, Lord. Remove every distraction, every deception, every dullness of heart. Let the fire of conviction fall.

God, we don't want hype; we want holiness. We don't want comfort; we want Christ. We don't want religion; we want revival. Start with us. Begin in our hearts. Shake what needs to be shaken, and awaken what has grown cold.

Use this work for your glory, Father. Let it bear fruit in this generation. In Jesus' mighty name I pray. Amen.

CHAPTER 1: **Wake Up**

ROM 13:11 KJV

"And that, knowing the time, that now it is high time to awake out of sleep: for now is our salvation nearer than when we believed."

The trumpet is sounding, and many still do not hear it. The call of God in this hour is not subtle; it is urgent. The world is asleep in deception, and tragically, so is much of the church. We live in a time of unprecedented access to truth, yet we are lulled by comfort, convenience, and compromise.

Romans 13:11 is not a suggestion; it is a Spirit-breathed wake-up call. Paul is not speaking to the world in this verse. He is speaking to believers. To the church. To those who already profess faith in Christ. And what does he say? "Now it is high time to awake out of sleep."

What is this sleep? It is spiritual dullness. It is the state of going through the motions of religion while the soul drifts farther and farther from true intimacy with God. It is prayer without power. Worship without surrender. Attendance without repentance. It is a numbing of the spirit beneath layers of distraction, pride, and unconfessed sin.

We have become so busy with life that we are missing life himself. We scroll past his voice. We multitask our devotion. We sip spiritual milk when we are called to eat the meat of the word. And all the while, the signs of the times are screaming. The earth groans. Evil accelerates. The darkness thickens. And still many slumber.

The enemy doesn't need to destroy you if he can distract you. He doesn't have to persecute you if he can pacify you. Spiritual sleep feels safe. It feels familiar. But it is deadly. Because salvation is nearer now than when we first believed. Jesus is coming. Time is running out.

We must wake up to righteousness. Wake up to repentance. Wake up to the harvest that is perishing while we entertain ourselves to death. We must rise up in the power of the Holy Ghost and cast off the works of darkness.

To wake up means to cast off the slumber of sin. To repent for our apathy. To cry out for oil in our lamps. To watch and pray. To fast and weep. To intercede for the lost. To walk in the Spirit and not fulfill the lust of the flesh.

Now is the time. Not tomorrow. Not after you finish your plans. Not when life gets easier. Not when you feel like it. Now. Today is the day of salvation. Now is the hour of awakening. The King is coming, and he's not returning for a drowsy bride. He's coming for those who are burning, watching, and ready.

Let this chapter shake you. Let the word cut you. Let the Spirit convict you. If you've been sleeping, wake up. If you've grown numb, repent. If you've wandered, return. Jesus is near. And this is the moment to be found faithful.

The alarm has sounded. Heaven is watching. The time is now.

EPH 5:14 KJV

"Wherefore he saith, Awake thou that sleepest, and arise from the dead, and Christ shall give thee light."

This is not just poetry; it is a prophetic command. Christ is calling his bride to arise, to leave behind the graveclothes of sin and complacency, and to walk in his blazing light. The hour is too late for delay.

TRUMPET CALL

- ✆ Wake up, church! The bridegroom is at the door.

- ✆ Shake off the chains of slumber, and light your lamp with oil from his Spirit.

- ✆ Refuse to be lulled by comfort—burn with holy fire.

- ✆ The King is coming—be awake, be watching, be ready!

CHAPTER 2: **The Last Days Are Here**

2 TIM 3:1–5 KJV

"This know also, that in the last days perilous times shall come. For men shall be lovers of their own selves, covetous, boasters, proud, blasphemers, disobedient to parents, unthankful, unholy, Without natural affection, trucebreakers, false accusers, incontinent, fierce, despisers of those that are good, Traitors, heady, highminded, lovers of pleasures more than lovers of God; Having a form of godliness, but denying the power thereof: from such turn away."

We are no longer waiting for the last days; they are here. The apostle Paul's words to Timothy are not a prediction for a distant future; they are a description of our present reality. Every phrase in this passage reads like the headlines of today's world. What was once unthinkable is now celebrated. What was once warned against is now welcomed.

Notice that Paul begins by saying, "This know also." This is not optional knowledge. This is not a maybe. The church is commanded to discern the time, to recognize the hour. Yet so many believers today are unaware, apathetic, or even deceived into thinking we have plenty of time. We don't. The time is short.

Perilous times have come. We live in a generation consumed by self. Lovers of their own selves. Our culture celebrates self-love, self-expression, and self-gratification, but the word of God warns that self is the enemy of surrender. A life centered on self cannot be centered on Christ.

These verses are not describing atheists; they are describing people who wear the name of God but deny the power that comes from knowing him. Paul is talking about people who go to church, say the right things, but live in secret rebellion. A form of godliness without fire. Religion without repentance. Services without surrender.

This is a warning to the church. Not to blend in with culture, but to stand out in holiness. To return to preaching sin, judgment, righteousness, and the cross. To stop entertaining goats and start feeding sheep. To stop being silent while the world burns.

God is not calling us to fear, but to faith. Not to hide, but to shine. We must be a people who walk in power, not just noise. We must be rooted in the word, led by the Spirit, and set apart from the world. The time for casual Christianity is over.

The last days are not on the horizon; they are in our face. This is the final hour. We must examine our hearts: are we living with urgency, or have we been lulled to sleep? Are we clinging to the truth, or compromising for comfort? Do we fear God, or do we fear man?

The Lord is looking for a remnant—those who have not bowed to Baal, who have not traded truth for applause. Those who still burn for righteousness, who still believe in holiness, who still preach repentance, who still expect revival.

This is not a call to panic. It is a call to purity. A call to preparation. A call to preach the gospel like never before. Because these are the days the prophets spoke of. These are the times Jesus warned about. And this is the moment we were born for.

Wake up, church. The last days are here.

Matt 24:12–13 KJV

"And because iniquity shall abound, the love of many shall wax cold. But he that shall endure unto the end, the same shall be saved."

TRUMPET CALL

- ↝ The last days are not coming—they are here.
- ↝ Shake off compromise and endure in holiness.
- ↝ Refuse to let your love grow cold.
- ↝ Preach the gospel, shine the light, and stand firm until the end.

CHAPTER 3: Lukewarm Will Not Last

Rev 3:15–16 KJV

"I know thy works, that thou art neither cold nor hot: I would thou wert cold or hot. So then because thou art lukewarm, and neither cold nor hot, I will spue thee out of my mouth."

This is one of the most sobering warnings in the entire Bible—Jesus Christ himself telling the church, "I will spit you out." Not because they were evil, but because they were lukewarm. Not because they were openly rebellious, but because they were half committed, half awake, halfhearted.

Lukewarm faith is deceptive. It feels safe. It mimics obedience. It shows up on Sundays. It might even volunteer or tithe. But deep down, it lacks fire. It lacks surrender. It lives off past encounters and religious routine, not off the presence and power of God.

Jesus wasn't speaking to unbelievers here. He was addressing the church in Laodicea, a church that looked alive, that thought it was rich and needed nothing. But Jesus said they were "wretched, miserable, poor, blind, and naked." Why? Because they had grown comfortable. They had grown casual with the holy. They had become content with the form of religion but denied the urgency of full surrender.

Lukewarm believers say "Lord" but live like they're in control. They sing about the cross but avoid carrying their own. They want the blessings of God without the burden of obedience. But Jesus is not fooled. He knows our works. He sees the temperature of our hearts.

This is the condition of much of the modern church. We have churches filled with people who know the words but not the word. Who clap for Jesus but won't follow him to Calvary. Who say "amen" but won't say "I repent." And Jesus is not impressed. He is nauseated.

He doesn't want half. He wants all. He doesn't want Sunday-only faith; he wants daily obedience. He doesn't want casual love; he wants blazing devotion.

And the warning is clear: lukewarm will not last. Lukewarm will not survive the shaking. Lukewarm will not endure the persecution that is coming. Lukewarm will not hear, "Well done." Lukewarm will be spewed out.

So what's the answer? Repentance. Zeal. Fire. Return to your first love. Fast. Pray. Weep. Ask God to baptize you with holy fire again. Get back into his word. Remove every idol. Reject every compromise. Make no provision for the flesh. Stop comparing your walk to lukewarm Christians around you. Compare it to the call of Jesus.

Now is not the time to play church. Now is not the time to live half saved. Now is not the time to flirt with sin and hope for mercy. Jesus is coming back, and he's not coming for a lukewarm bride. He's coming for one who is burning with love, set apart in holiness, awake and alive in him.

If you've grown cold, cry out for fire. If you've drifted, run back. If you've been going through the motions, stop. Get on your face. The mercy of God is still available. The fire of God is still falling.

But you must decide. Because the lukewarm will not last. Not in this hour. Not in what's coming. Not in eternity. Choose fire. Choose surrender. Choose Jesus, fully and forever.

Now is the time.

MATT 24:42 KJV

Watch therefore: for ye know not what hour your Lord doth come.

Lukewarmness is not just dangerous—it is deadly. Jesus is not returning for those who are half awake. He is returning for a bride who is burning, alert, and ready.

TRUMPET CALL

- Lukewarm will not last—choose fire or be spewed out.
- Refuse casual faith—embrace holy zeal.
- Watch, pray, repent, and burn with devotion.
- The bridegroom is coming soon—let your lamp be full and your fire blazing!

DECLARATION

I refuse to live lukewarm.

I will not be half committed, half awake, or halfhearted.

I choose fire. I choose surrender. I choose Jesus—fully and forever.

I will keep my lamp burning, my heart watching, and my life ready for the return of my King.

CHAPTER 4: **Calling Evil Good**

We are living in a time where the line between truth and deception has been intentionally blurred. The words of the prophet Isaiah are more relevant today than ever: "Woe unto them that call evil good, and good evil." It is not just that evil exists; it is that it is now applauded, celebrated, and institutionalized. And worse, many who claim the name of Christ remain silent.

> Isa 5:20 KJV
>
> *"Woe unto them that call evil good, and good evil; that put darkness for light, and light for darkness; that put bitter for sweet, and sweet for bitter!"*

> Amos 5:14–15 KJV
>
> *"Seek good, and not evil, that ye may live: and so the Lord, the God of hosts, shall be with you, as ye have spoken. Hate the evil, and love the good, and establish judgment in the gate: it may be that the Lord God of hosts will be gracious unto the remnant of Joseph."*

We were warned that in the last days, deception would increase. And one of the most dangerous forms of deception is not atheism; it's false Christianity. A religion that looks like truth but lacks repentance. A gospel that comforts the sinner but never convicts. A message that promises heaven but never demands holiness. This is the climate Isaiah was prophesying into—a generation that flips the moral compass and silences the voice of righteousness.

2 TIM 4:3–4 KJV

"For the time will come when they will not endure sound doctrine; but after their own lusts shall they heap to them-selves teachers, having itching ears; And they shall turn away their ears from the truth, and shall be turned unto fables."

Today, evil is not just tolerated, it's mainstream. Sin parades in the streets while holiness is mocked. Perversion is called love. Abortion is called healthcare. Rebellion is called bravery. And if you speak the truth, you are labeled hateful, judgmental, or extreme. We now live in a world where the clearer your conviction, the more likely you'll be canceled.

ROM 1:28–32 KJV

"And even as they did not like to retain God in their knowl-edge, God gave them over to a reprobate mind, to do those things which are not convenient; Being filled with all un-righteousness, fornication, wickedness, covetousness, ma-liciousness; full of envy, murder, debate, deceit, malignity; whisperers, Backbiters, haters of God, despiteful, proud, boasters, inventors of evil things, disobedient to parents, Without understanding, covenantbreakers, without natu-ral affection, implacable, unmerciful: Who knowing the judgment of God, that they which commit such things are worthy of death, not only do the same, but have pleasure in them that do them."

MATT 24:12 KJV

"And because iniquity shall abound, the love of many shall wax cold."

But this isn't just a problem in the culture; it's a crisis in the church. Many pastors have laid down their swords in exchange for applause. Sermons are filled with jokes, motivation, and positive affirmations, but are void of power, truth, and the fear of the Lord. We have traded altar calls for stage shows, holiness for hype, and repentance for relatability.

God's word has not changed. What he called sin in Genesis, he still calls sin in Revelation. Holiness is still the standard. Repentance is still required. Hell is still real. And the cross is still the only way to salvation. Yet we live in a generation that wants to rewrite the Bible to fit their feelings rather than crucify their feelings to obey the Bible.

Isaiah's warning begins with "Woe," a divine cry of grief and judgment. To call evil good is not just a mistake; it is rebellion. It is shaking your fist at heaven and declaring your own standard. And make no mistake, judgment will come, not just on the world, but on the house of God.

It's time to return to preaching the full counsel of God. We must preach sin, hell, holiness, the blood, the cross, and the soon return of Christ. We must preach the fear of the Lord, not in a way that pushes people away, but in a way that compels them to fall at his feet. Because without the fear of God, there is no true repentance.

The church must no longer be silent while evil advances. We are not called to go with the flow; we are called to resist the tide. To be salt and light. To stand up and speak out. Not in hatred, but in holy love. Because love without truth is deception, and truth without love is brutality. But when truth and love come together, people are changed.

The fear of man has silenced too many pulpits. But we were not called to please man. We were called to preach Jesus—crucified, risen, and returning. We were called to confront darkness. To tear down strongholds. To expose the works of the enemy with the blazing light of truth.

This chapter is not just a commentary; it's a call to arms. A spiritual awakening. A prophetic rebuke and a loving plea. Do not participate in the evil of this generation. Do not water down the gospel. Do not trade truth for popularity.

Woe to those who call evil good. But blessed are those who stand for righteousness in an age of compromise.

Let the fire of God burn in your bones. Let the word be like a hammer in your mouth. Let the Spirit of truth rise up in boldness. We are not here to be liked; we are here to be holy.

Now is the time to speak. Now is the time to stand. Now is the time to call good good and evil evil, no matter the cost.

EPH 5:11 KJV

"And have no fellowship with the unfruitful works of darkness, but rather reprove them."

This is not a suggestion; it is a command. The church is not called to blend in with the world, but to expose its darkness with the light of Christ. To be silent in the face of evil is to consent to it. To compromise with wickedness is to betray holiness.

TRUMPET CALL

- Now is the time for the church to rise in holiness and truth.
- Refuse to call evil good—declare the standard of God without fear.
- Do not be silent. Do not compromise. The Spirit is raising a remnant that will shine with boldness.
- Let your voice carry the fire of heaven and your life bear the fruit of holiness.

CHAPTER 5: **The Cry for Holiness**

HEB 12:14 KJV

"Follow peace with all men, and holiness, without which no man shall see the Lord."

The cry for holiness is almost forgotten in our day. Yet, it is the one cry heaven will never ignore. Without holiness, no man shall see the Lord. That is not optional. That is not negotiable. That is the word of God.

We've built a Christianity that substitutes hype for holiness. We fill the altars with noise but not with repentance. We have programs polished and lights perfected, but the presence is absent because the altar of holiness is forsaken.

Holiness is not a denominational preference. It is not "legalism." It is not outdated. Holiness is the very nature of God. And he has called his people to reflect him.

First Peter 1:16 declares, *"Be ye holy; for I am holy."*

This is the standard. Not perfection by human effort, but purity through surrender. Not a checklist of rules, but a consecrated heart burning for the Lord.

Holiness Misunderstood

Some equate holiness with outward appearance. Others confuse it with self-righteousness. But true holiness is Christlikeness. It is a life laid down. It is a vessel emptied of pride, lust, greed, and selfishness, so it may be filled with the Spirit of God.

Holiness is not bondage. Holiness is freedom. It is the breaking of chains. It is walking in victory over the flesh. It is living unashamed in the presence of a holy God.

The enemy mocks holiness because he fears its power. A holy people cannot be bought, cannot be swayed, cannot be silenced. They carry the authority of heaven.

The Cost of Holiness

Holiness will cost you something. It may cost you friends. It may cost you opportunities. It will certainly cost you to compromise. But what it gives you is infinitely greater: intimacy with God, clarity of spirit, and authority in prayer.

We cannot afford to preach a gospel without holiness. We cannot raise another generation that thinks salvation means forgiveness without transformation.

The call is clear: without holiness, no man shall see the Lord.

A Church Without Holiness

Why are our churches powerless? Because we have traded holiness for popularity. We want acceptance from the world more than we want anointing from heaven. We want the applause of men more than the approval of God.

But the Bible says judgment must begin at the house of God. The Spirit is cleansing his bride. He is raising up a remnant that will not bow to Baal, that will not sell out to sin, that will not dilute the message.

The cry of this hour is not, "Give us more lights." It is, "Give us holiness."

Wake Up, Church

The days of lukewarm faith are over. God is drawing a line. On one side stands compromise, on the other stands consecration. You must choose.

Do not be deceived: grace does not excuse sin; grace empowers holiness. Mercy is not a license to continue in darkness; it is the call to walk in light.

This is the hour to return to the altar, to rend our hearts, to repent with tears, and to pursue the one who is holy, holy, holy.

TRUMPET CALL

- ✺ Return to holiness.
- ✺ Cast off compromise.
- ✺ Purify your heart, your home, your ministry.
- ✺ Without holiness, you will not see the Lord.

The trumpet is sounding. The fire is calling. Holiness must be restored.

REFLECT

- Have I confused grace with permission to sin?
- Do I desire the applause of men more than the approval of God?
- Am I willing to pay the price to walk in holiness?

DECLARATION

I will walk in holiness, not by my own strength, but by the power of the Holy Spirit.

I will not bow to compromise.

I will not water down the call of God.

I will live pure, consecrated, and burning for my King.

HEB 12:14 KJV

"Follow peace with all men, and holiness, without which no man shall see the Lord."

CHAPTER 6: **Return to Holiness**

1 PET 1:15–16 KJV

"But as he which hath called you is holy, so be ye holy in all manner of conversation; Because it is written, Be ye holy; for I am holy."

Holiness is not a suggestion; it is a command from the living God. The same God who thundered on Mount Sinai, who filled the temple with glory, who struck down Ananias and Sapphira for lying in the New Testament—that same holy God has called his people to be set apart.

The tragedy of our time is that holiness has been traded for popularity. Reverence has been replaced with entertainment. The sacred has been profaned, and yet we wonder why revival tarries. God has not changed, but we have. And if we are to walk in the power of the early church, we must return to the posture of early obedience.

"Be ye holy" is not merely about avoiding sin. It's about becoming like him—in purity, in speech, in motive, in devotion. It's about fleeing not just what is evil but even what is common, choosing the narrow way that few dare to walk. Holiness means cutting off what defiles, casting down every thought that exalts itself against the knowledge of God, and living in a continual state of repentance and consecration.

There is a reason Scripture calls it "the beauty of holiness" (Ps 29:2). Because there is nothing more radiant than a life fully yielded to God. A life that burns with integrity, that glows with clean hands and a pure heart, that bows when no one is looking and weeps over the sins that no one else sees.

Yet today, how rare is this call from the pulpits? Instead, we hear soft sermons that stroke the flesh and leave the soul untouched. But without holiness, no man shall see the Lord (Heb 12:14). That is not metaphor; it is truth. Heaven is not for the casual believer, but for the crucified one. The one who dies daily, who wars against the flesh, who lives as though Jesus might return at any moment—because he will.

It's time to restore the altar. To tear down the Asherah poles of compromise. To cast out the idols we've hidden in our tents. We must fall on our faces like Isaiah, who cried, "Woe is me! For I am undone . . . for mine eyes have seen the King!" (Isa 6:5). And only when the coal from the altar touches our lips will we rise up to speak again with authority.

Holiness is not legalism. It is liberty. It is the freedom to live unchained by sin. It is the joy of a clean conscience. It is the power of walking blameless in a perverse generation, shining like stars in the darkness.

This generation needs a holy church. Not trendy. Not clever. Holy. A church that trembles at his word. That doesn't need the smoke machines because it has the glory cloud. That doesn't need catchy slogans because it carries the weight of heaven. That doesn't flirt with the world because it is betrothed to one.

Friend, the Lord is coming back for a bride without spot or wrinkle. Not a church with perfect branding or an Instagram following, but a remnant clothed in white, who has washed her garments in the blood of the Lamb and kept herself ready. Will you be found among her?

Let us not settle for near-holiness. For part-time purity. Let us rise in this hour and return—fully, wholly, fiercely—to the holiness of God. For only in that fire will we be truly set free.

HEB 12:14 KJV

"Follow peace with all men, and holiness, without which no man shall see the Lord."

Holiness is not optional for the believer. It is the very evidence that Christ dwells within us. Without it, we are blind guides; but with it, we shine as a testimony of his transforming power.

TRUMPET CALL

- ↵ Return to holiness! Tear down every idol and cleanse your garments in the blood of the Lamb.
- ↵ Refuse to settle for casual Christianity —walk in consecration.
- ↵ Let your life be marked by purity, integrity, and the fear of the Lord.
- ↵ The King is coming for a bride without spot or wrinkle —be ready!

CHAPTER 7: **The Gospel of the Kingdom vs. the Gospel of Success**

MATT 6:33 KJV

"But seek ye first the kingdom of God, and his righteousness; and all these things shall be added unto you."

The gospel of the kingdom is not the same as the gospel of success. One is built on surrender, while the other is built on self. One points to the cross, while the other to comfort. One produces disciples, while the other produces consumers.

The true gospel of Jesus Christ calls us to die to ourselves. To pick up our cross. To follow him no matter the cost. It does not promise ease; it promises eternal life through the narrow road of obedience.

MATT 7:13–14 KJV

"Enter ye in at the strait gate: for wide is the gate, and broad is the way, that leadeth to destruction, and many there be which go in thereat:

Because strait is the gate, and narrow is the way, which leadeth unto life, and few there be that find it."

But the gospel being preached in many churches today says, "Come to Jesus, and you'll be rich." "Come to Jesus, and your problems will go away." "Come to Jesus, and get your breakthrough."

Jesus is not a means to an end; he is the end. He is not a tool for your dreams; he is Lord. He didn't come to pad your lifestyle; he came to crucify your flesh.

LUKE 9:23 KJV

"And he said to them all, If any man will come after me, let him deny himself, and take up his cross daily, and follow me."

The gospel of success exalts man. The gospel of the kingdom exalts the King.

We have exchanged the Lion of Judah for a life coach. We've turned the house of prayer into a center for personal development. But the gospel is not self-help; it is self-denial. It is not about "your best life now"—it is about laying your life down for the sake of the gospel.

2 TIM 4:3–4 KJV

"For the time will come when they will not endure sound doctrine; but after their own lusts shall they heap to themselves teachers, having itching ears;

And they shall turn away their ears from the truth, and shall be turned unto fables."

We are in that time now. The church is full of itching ears and teachers who are willing to scratch them for a price.

But God is raising up voices that cannot be bought. Preachers who are not for hire. Watchmen who cry out from the wall, even when no one wants to hear it.

The gospel of the kingdom turns the world upside down. It doesn't promise luxury; it promises persecution. It doesn't offer popularity; it demands holiness. It doesn't magnify men; it magnifies the Lamb.

ROM 14:17 KJV

"For the kingdom of God is not meat and drink; but righteousness, and peace, and joy in the Holy Ghost."

The gospel of the kingdom is the message Jesus preached. And it is the message that must return to the pulpits, no matter the cost.

We do not need another brand of Christianity. We need the fire of the kingdom. We need the cross. We need the truth. And we need to repent for the counterfeit we've embraced.

Let the gospel be preached in power again.

Let the kingdom come.

TRUMPET CALL

- ✧ I reject the gospel of comfort. I will not trade the cross for applause.

- ✧ I choose the narrow way. I choose righteousness over riches. I choose Jesus over every earthly promise.

- ✧ I am not here to build my kingdom; I am here to see his kingdom come.

- ✧ I will preach the truth, live the truth, and endure whatever it costs.

- ✧ I belong to the King.

- ✧ *Now is the time.*

CHAPTER 8: **Repentance in the House of God**

1 Pet 4:17 KJV

"For the time is come that judgment must begin at the house of God: and if it first begin at us, what shall the end be of them that obey not the gospel of God?"

The church cries out for revival, but heaven cries out for repentance. We long for power, but neglect purity. We pray for glory, but bypass the altar.

God will not anoint what he cannot cleanse. He will not revive what refuses to repent. He is not impressed with emotional services that never lead to spiritual change.

The greatest need in the house of God is not new programs, bigger buildings, or better branding. The greatest need is brokenness. A holy return to the altar where tears are shed, hearts are pierced, and sin is forsaken.

Joel 2:12–13 KJV

"Therefore also now, saith the Lord, turn ye even to me with all your heart, and with fasting, and with weeping, and with mourning:

And rend your heart, and not your garments, and turn

unto the Lord your God: for he is gracious and merciful,
slow to anger, and of great kindness, and repenteth him
of the evil."

God is not looking for performance; he is looking for surrender. Not outward gestures, but inward transformation. We must rend our hearts. We must fall on our faces again. We must stop pointing fingers at the world and start weeping over the condition of the church.

We have traded conviction for comfort. We have replaced tears of repentance with shouts of hype. But heaven is not moved by noise; it is moved by surrender.

Repentance is not a onetime event; it is the posture of the bride who longs to be pure for her bridegroom. A heart that stays low before God. A soul that grieves over sin. A people that cry out, "Search me, O God, and know my heart."

REV 2:16 KJV

"Repent; or else I will come unto thee quickly, and will
fight against them with the sword of my mouth."

Jesus did not say this to a pagan nation; he said it to his church. He is calling his people back to holiness. Back to the truth. Back to the altar. And he is coming quickly.

What we tolerate today will become chains tomorrow. What we excuse in the pulpit will multiply in the pews. And what we refuse to repent of will be judged.

The sins we've excused must now be exposed. The hidden idols must be cast down. The fear of man must bow to the fear of God. There is no awakening without repentance. There is no revival without return.

ACTS 3:19 KJV

*"Repent ye therefore, and be converted, that your sins may
be blotted out, when the times of refreshing shall come
from the presence of the Lord."*

The refreshing comes, but only after repentance. The Spirit moves
where he is honored, not where he is mocked. And a church that
refuses to repent forfeits the glory of God.

We want the fire to fall, but we have removed the altar. We want
miracles, but we don't want to fast. We want overflow, but refuse to
empty ourselves first.

This is the hour to cry aloud and spare not. To call sin what God
calls it. To preach with tears in our eyes and fire in our bones. To
tremble at his word.

It is not the world that is holding back revival. It is the pride of the
church. The stage has replaced the secret place. Performance has
replaced purity.

Repentance must return, not as a moment, but as a mantle. We
must wear it daily. We must walk in it humbly. We must preach
it boldly.

Let it begin in us. Let the tears fall again. Let the altar be rebuilt.
Let the bride make herself ready.

TRUMPET CALL

- The time for casual Christianity is over.

- The trumpet is sounding from the altar, not to entertain, but to awaken. The Holy Spirit is calling the bride to prepare herself. The Master is at the door. The fire must fall, but only where the altar is rebuilt.

- Church, repent. Saints, return. Watchmen, warn.

- Let the priests weep between the porch and the altar.

- Let pastors cry out again. Let intercessors groan. Let worship leaders sing songs of surrender, not self.

- Let pulpits be purified. Let pews be pierced. Let the house of God fall on its face.

- *Now is the time.*

CHAPTER 9: **Ichabod and the Abandoned Altar**

1 Sam 4:21 KJV

"And she named the child Ichabod, saying, The glory is departed from Israel: because the ark of God was taken, and because of her father in law and her husband."

"Ichabod." One word—and everything changed. The glory had left. The presence of God was no longer with his people. And the worst part? Many didn't even realize it.

We have built churches without altars. Services without surrender. Worship without reverence. And like Israel, we continue moving forward in form, but void of fire.

There is no greater tragedy than a church that still gathers but no longer hosts his presence. A people who still sing but no longer tremble. A pulpit that still preaches but no longer weeps.

We can lose the glory and keep the crowd. We can lose the anointing and still keep the programs. We can abandon the altar and still attract the masses. But the heavens know. And hell is not threatened.

Ezek 10:18 KJV

"Then the glory of the Lord departed from off the threshold

of the house, and stood over the cherubims."

The prophet Ezekiel saw what many failed to see—the glory of the Lord departing the temple. And yet today, many churches are still functioning under Ichabod—with fog machines but no fear of God, polished sermons but no power.

Where is the altar of brokenness? Where are the groanings? Where are the watchmen who cry out between the porch and the altar?

We have confused momentum with revival. Noise with nearness. But the question of this hour is not, "How big is your ministry?," but, "Is God still in the midst of it?"

When the altar is abandoned, the glory departs. When repentance is replaced with entertainment, heaven closes its windows. When the fear of the Lord is dismissed, "Ichabod" is written across the doorpost.

JER 6:10 KJV

"To whom shall I speak, and give warning, that they may hear? behold, their ear is uncircumcised, and they cannot hearken: behold, the word of the Lord is unto them a reproach; they have no delight in it."

The modern church has stopped delighting in the word. We pick the parts that please the crowd and skip the ones that confront sin. We have catered to goats and neglected the sheep. And the fire has gone out.

You cannot microwave the glory. You cannot manufacture holiness. The fire only falls on the altar, and the altar must be rebuilt.

Let every Ichabod house repent. Let every platform that replaced purity be cleansed. Let every leader who bowed to applause return to the fear of the Lord.

Ichabod is not just a warning. It is a wake-up call. The glory left, but it can return. The fire faded, but it can fall again.

But it begins with the altar. The sacrifice. The tears. The hunger. The obedience.

If we want the glory back, we must want God more than growth. We must want purity more than popularity. We must want holiness more than hype.

Let the cry rise again: "Lord, take not thy Holy Spirit from me!" Let the church fall on its face again and say, "We will not move without your presence."

Ichabod ends where repentance begins.

The church cannot afford to look successful while living defeated. We cannot keep pretending the glory is here when we know deep down it has departed.

We dance on stages while angels weep. We host conferences while heaven waits. And all the while, the fire that once marked us has become a flicker or gone out altogether.

This is not about emotion; it's about presence. The kind that convicts. That purifies. That shakes buildings and breaks chains.

We must rebuild the altar. Tear down the idols. Cancel the show. Get low again. Let the incense of prayer rise. Let the tears of intercession fall.

Ichabod is not the end, unless we ignore it. But if we hear the trumpet, if we fall on our faces, if we rend our hearts, then the fire can fall again.

TRUMPET CALL

- ✺ Has the glory departed, and no one noticed?

- ✺ The fire falls on the altar, but we've removed it for a stage. The fear of God has been exchanged for the praise of man. It is time to return.

- ✺ Let every Ichabod house be shaken. Let every platform be purified. Let the bride awaken and tremble again before the King of Glory.

- ✺ The glory of God is not a feeling; it is the weight of his presence. And without it, we are powerless.

- ✺ *Now is the time.*

DECLARATION

We will not be a people who carry the name of God but lack his presence.

We renounce every idol, every performance, and every pretense that has replaced the fear of the Lord.

We rebuild the altar.

We return to the fire.

We welcome the glory.

Let Ichabod be reversed in our generation.

Let the church burn again with holiness, truth, and power.

We will not move without you, Lord. We will not settle for a form without fire.

The glory will return—because we return.

CHAPTER 10: **The Compromised Pulpit and the Silenced Prophets**

JER 6:14 KJV

"They have healed also the hurt of the daughter of my people slightly, saying, Peace, peace; when there is no peace."

The pulpit was never meant to be a stage for entertainers. It was meant to be a platform for truth. But many who once carried fire now carry fear. Fear of offense. Fear of losing followers. Fear of being labeled unloving.

And so, in pulpits across the land, truth has been replaced with tolerance, conviction with comfort. Prophets have been silenced, not by martyrdom, but by applause. The word of the Lord has been edited to appease the crowd.

But heaven is not applauding. The Spirit is grieved. The glory is withheld. Because truth has fallen in the streets, and compromise now wears a collar.

2 TIM 4:3–4 KJV

"For the time will come when they will not endure sound doctrine; but after their own lusts shall they heap to themselves teachers, having itching ears."

And they shall turn away their ears from the truth, and shall be turned unto fables.

This isn't a prophecy for the future; it's a description of now. Many churches are full, but the truth is scarce. Sermons are crafted for comfort, not for confrontation. And the prophets who cry out are labeled divisive.

But God never called his messengers to be popular. He called them to be faithful. He called them to cry aloud and spare not. To confront sin, not cozy up to it.

ISAIAH 30:10 KJV

"Which say to the seers, See not; and to the prophets, Prophesy not unto us right things, speak unto us smooth things, prophesy deceits."

This is the request of a rebellious people. "Tell us what we want to hear. Preach to our preferences. Entertain us, but don't expose us." And sadly, many preachers have obliged.

But God is raising up voices again. Uncompromising. Unashamed. Unmuzzled. They will not be bought. They will not be silenced. They fear God more than man. And they burn with the word of the Lord.

We don't need more influencers. We need more intercessors. We don't need more celebrity pastors. We need more weeping watchmen. Men and women who will stand between the porch and the altar and cry out for a compromised generation.

The pulpit must be cleansed. The prophets must arise. The word must thunder again. And the church must repent for trading power for popularity.

JER 23:29 KJV

"Is not my word like as a fire? saith the Lord; and like a hammer that breaketh the rock in pieces?"

We don't need soft speech. We need holy fire. We don't need sugar-coated sermons. We need the sword of the Spirit. The church will not survive the days ahead without a return to truth.

Let the compromised pulpit be shaken. Let the silenced prophets roar again. Let truth rise and the fear of the Lord return.

The hour is too late for pleasantries. We need preachers who still tremble. Prophets who still weep. Saints who still kneel.

If we want revival, we must restore the roar of the uncompromising word.

TRUMPET CALL

- ✺ The hour of silence is over.

- ✺ The Spirit is sounding the trumpet—calling forth the voices that will not bow. The days of sugarcoated sermons are ending.

- ✺ Let the fire return to the pulpit. Let the word roar again. Let the prophets speak.

- ✺ *Now is the time.*

CHAPTER 11: **The Great Falling Away Has Already Begun**

2 Thess 2:3 KJV

"Let no man deceive you by any means: for that day shall not come, except there come a falling away first, and that man of sin be revealed, the son of perdition."

We are no longer on the brink of the great falling away; we are knee-deep in it. Churches that once stood firm now shake under the pressure of culture. The word of God has been edited for comfort. The cross has been sanitized. The gospel has been downsized. And the altars have been replaced with stages.

The great falling away is not just people leaving the church. It is people staying in the church while their hearts depart from the truth. It is the slow erosion of holiness, the compromise of doctrine, and the casual dismissal of sin. It is a generation that claims to love Jesus but refuses to obey him.

1 Tim 4:1 KJV

"Now the Spirit speaketh expressly, that in the latter times some shall depart from the faith, giving heed to seducing spirits, and doctrines of devils."

Seducing spirits don't wear horns; they wear smiles. They preach in pulpits and sing on platforms. They say what itching ears want to hear: that sin is not so serious, that love is tolerant of everything, that God will never judge. And the church, instead of rebuking the lies, has welcomed them with open arms.

We have mistaken compromise for compassion. We've confused popularity with anointing. And we've forgotten that Jesus flipped tables in the temple not to be controversial, but to cleanse what man had corrupted.

Apostasy isn't always loud. Sometimes it looks like excellence without consecration. Activity without intimacy. Growth without repentance. It's when the outward show continues, but the Spirit has departed.

REV 3:15–16 KJV

"I know thy works, that thou art neither cold nor hot: I would thou wert cold or hot. So then because thou art lukewarm, and neither cold nor hot, I will spue thee out of my mouth."

Lukewarm faith is the breeding ground of the great falling away. It sings but does not surrender. It attends but does not obey. It speaks of God but lives without him. And Jesus says he will spew it out.

Where are the voices crying out in the wilderness? Where are the watchmen who still weep for the compromise in the camp? Where are the preachers who care more about souls than self-promotion?

The great falling away isn't happening because sinners are sinning; it's happening because the saints have stopped standing. We've gone silent when we should have roared. We've blended in when we were called to stand out. We've bowed to culture instead of burning for Christ.

MATT 24:12 KJV

"And because iniquity shall abound, the love of many shall wax cold."

Love grows cold when truth is abandoned. And truth is often abandoned when fear of man outweighs fear of God. But now is not the time for fear; it's the time to rise in holy boldness.

The Lord is looking for a remnant, not polished, not perfect, but pure. Those who tremble at his word, who refuse to compromise, and who still burn with first-love fire. Those who have not bowed to Baal or kissed the idols of this world.

HEB 3:12–13 KJV

"Take heed, brethren, lest there be in any of you an evil heart of unbelief, in departing from the living God. But exhort one another daily . . . lest any of you be hardened through the deceitfulness of sin."

This is the time for daily exhortation, not casual conversation. We must call one another higher, warn of deception, and weep over the state of the church. Judgment is at the door, and eternity hangs in the balance.

Let every preacher strip away the polish and preach repentance. Let every saint fall on their face again. Let every church burn the idols and rebuild the altar. This is not a game. This is not a phase. This is the separation of wheat and tares.

The great falling away has already begun, but so has the call to return. Choose now whom you will serve. Not in word, but in action. Not in name, but in nature. Let there be no mixture, no middle ground, no more delay.

The bride must awaken. The fire must be stoked. The remnant must arise. And the church must remember what it means to fear the Lord again.

REFLECTIVE QUESTIONS

- Have I grown numb to the slow drift of compromise around me?

- Am I still burning with first-love fire, or have I grown cold?

- What false teachings or cultural lies have I allowed to shape my faith?

- Would I still follow Jesus if it meant losing my reputation, platform, or comfort?

- Have I departed from the altar while pretending to still carry the fire?

- Am I living in a way that proves I'm ready for the Lord's return?

CHAPTER 12: **Return to the Altar**

There was a time when the altar meant everything to the church. When men and women trembled at the presence of God, and wept over their sins before daring to rise from their knees.

Now, in many places, the altar has become ornamental—a stage piece. The sacred has become ceremonial, and the fire has faded from the hearts of God's people.

But the Spirit is calling again. Return to the altar, not in ritual, but in surrender. Not in form, but in fire.

JOEL 2:13 KJV

"And rend your heart, and not your garments."

The Lord is no longer impressed by outward displays. He is not looking for religious theater; he is looking for the torn hearts of a people who are done pretending.

To "rend your heart" means to let the Spirit shatter everything that's fake. It means allowing the Lord to cut into the places you've been hiding. It's not a suggestion; it's a cry for total surrender.

In this hour, the church must move past image. Past charisma. Past presentation. And back to brokenness. The altar is not a photo op. It's the meeting place between God's judgment and his mercy.

He will not despise a broken and contrite heart. But he will resist the proud platforms we build for ourselves while calling them "ministry."

The heart must tear before the heavens open. There is no shortcut.

ROMANS 12:1 KJV

"Present your bodies a living sacrifice, holy, acceptable unto God."

Revival doesn't start with emotional hype; it starts with sacrifice. With blood on the altar. With something being laid down, not just lifted up in song.

The modern church is very good at asking God for blessings, but very poor at laying our lives down in worship. We treat his altar like a bargaining table, not a burning place.

To be a living sacrifice means we offer all: our habits, our words, our thoughts, our time, our reputation. It means saying, "God, consume me. Burn away what doesn't please you."

Only when something precious dies on the altar will fire fall. Until then, we have noise without power. Lights without glory. Churches without change.

Return to the altar, not with some of you. With all of you.

1 KINGS 18:30 KJV

"And he repaired the altar of the Lord that was broken down."

Before the fire fell at Mount Carmel, Elijah repaired the altar. That should tell us everything.

We cry out for God to move, but have we prepared a place for him? Not a service. Not a platform. An altar.

Altars are not for decoration. They are for death. The church must first repair the altar of prayer. The altar of repentance. The altar of reverence.

Elijah didn't need a crowd. He didn't need lights. He needed a place where the covenant of God was honored again. Once the altar was restored, *then* the fire fell.

Church, if we want fire in this generation, we must first rebuild the altar in our own hearts.

PROPHETIC INTERLUDE

The altar is calling. Not the one made by hand,
but the one that pierces the soul.

I am not waiting on the world to turn; I am waiting on
my people to return.

Where are those who will kneel again? Where are the
leaders who will fall on their faces instead of chasing
applause? Where are my watchmen who cry between
the porch and the altar?

Return to me, and I will return to you. Build me
a real altar, and I will send my fire.

CHAPTER 13: **Revive Us Again**

Ps 85:6 KJV

"Wilt thou not revive us again: that thy people may rejoice in thee?"

This is the cry of a desperate people.

Not a rehearsed prayer. Not a Sunday recital. But a cry. A broken, breathless, trembling cry that pierces the heavens and pleads with God:

"Revive us again."

Not entertain us. Not bless us. Not build our brand. Revive us.

The joy is gone because the fire is gone. The fire is gone because repentance is gone. And repentance is gone because we stopped being desperate.

But the Spirit is stirring. Something is shaking. And heaven is asking, "Will my people cry out again?"

God has never turned away a desperate heart. He's never ignored a soul who wept at his feet. He's never refused a remnant willing to burn again.

Revival isn't an event. It's not a date on the calendar. Revival is when the glory of God collides with the surrender of man. And right now—this very moment—he is searching for hearts that will fall to their knees and say, "I don't want to play church. I want the fire back."

The old paths are calling. The altars are groaning. The wells of revival are being uncapped. But only the hungry will drink.

You who are weary, dry, numb, and exhausted, cry out. Let the tears fall again. Let the word pierce again. Let the fire consume again.

Wilt thou not revive us again? The answer is *yes*.

But it begins with you.

Lord, revive me—not next year, not next week, but *now*.

> Ps 85:6 KJV
>
> *"Wilt thou not revive us again: that thy people may rejoice in thee?"*

Revival doesn't come through convenience. It comes through consecration. We have entertained the crowds but forgotten the cloud. We've streamlined the service but starved the altar. And now God is calling the remnant back to the sacred place where his glory can fall.

You cannot microwave a move of God. You cannot schedule the Spirit. Revival is not found in the lights, the set list, or the sermon; it's found in the secret place. It's born in the groanings of intercession and the raw repentance of a bride who misses her bridegroom.

Where are the watchmen who will weep between the porch and the altar? Where are the pastors who will tear up their sermon notes because the Spirit is breaking out? Where are the worshipers who sing until the heavens shake and the glory floods the room?

The Lord is looking, not for perfect people, but for desperate ones. Desperate enough to cancel the program. Desperate enough to shut the doors to everything but his presence. Desperate enough to lay down ego and agenda and cry out, "Lord, we're not leaving until you move!"

We don't need another church service. We need an upper room. We need a people so hungry for his presence that everything else fades. When revival breaks out, it doesn't care about our time slots or titles. It breaks the box. It invades the routine. It demands the altar.

God is restoring the awe. He is reigniting the fear of the Lord. He is calling us to tremble again at his word and fall again at his feet. The laughter of entertainment is being replaced by the tears of repentance. The shallow is giving way to the sacred.

And when he really comes, it won't be business as usual. The drunk will stumble into the sanctuary and get sober in the Spirit. The suicidal will throw away the pills. The addicted will be delivered. The backslidden will fall to their knees. Entire regions will shift under the weight of his glory.

This is not hype. It's holy. This is not manufactured. It's miraculous. And it's coming, but only to the people who prepare the altar.

So rise up, remnant. Rebuild the altar. Stoke the fire. Refuse to be satisfied with a shell of Christianity when Jesus paid for the full flame.

Revive us again, Lord, until the world sees you in us.

DECLARATION

- 🔥 I will not settle for dry religion.
- 🔥 I will not go another day without the fire of the Holy Spirit.
- 🔥 I will return to the altar until revival ignites in me.
- 🔥 I will cry out until my city is shaken.

CHAPTER 14: **Merchandising the Anointing**

2 PET 2:3 KJV

"And through covetousness shall they with feigned words make merchandise of you: whose judgment now of a long time lingereth not, and their damnation slumbereth not."

The things of God are not for sale.

Yet in our generation, the anointing has been branded. The gifts of the Spirit have been packaged. The gospel has been given a price tag.

They've taken the sacred and turned it into a strategy. They've taken the fire and made it into a feature. They've taken what was meant to be freely given and turned it into profit.

God never charged a hurting soul to be healed. Jesus never sold access to deliverance. The apostles didn't set up booths to sell the Holy Ghost.

And yet now, in this age of spiritual consumerism, we pay for "prophetic words," buy "mantles," and sponsor "revival"—as long as the cost is met.

This is not kingdom. This is corruption.

The church has forgotten how to freely give because it has forgotten how freely it received. It is one thing to support the laborer. It is another to merchandise the oil.

God will not allow his presence to be reduced to product. His glory is not a commodity. His anointing is not a marketing plan.

Judgment is coming to the spiritual merchants, unless they repent.

And to the remnant, he says: Don't touch it. Don't imitate it. Don't envy it.

Guard the oil. Purify the altar. And never put a price on what Jesus paid for in blood.

There is a cost to carrying the anointing, but it is not a financial one. It is a cost of consecration. A price of purity. A sacrifice of self. The anointing comes through the crushing, not through commerce.

When Simon the sorcerer tried to buy the power of the Holy Ghost, Peter rebuked him sharply for thinking that the gift of God could be purchased with money. That same rebuke rings loud in this hour. We have Simons in suits and pulpits. Platforms full of sorcery disguised as spirituality.

The Spirit of the Lord grieves when his presence is prostituted for clout. He is holy. He is not for hire. His fire is not a franchise. His power is not pay-per-view.

If Jesus were to walk through some churches today, he would do what he did in the temple—flip the tables, drive out the merchandisers, and cleanse his Father's house. And make no mistake, he is doing it again.

To the true remnant: do not sell out. Do not sell short. Do not be seduced. Hold the line. Preach the word. Guard the anointing like it's holy because it is.

You don't need a gimmick. You need the glory. You don't need a strategy. You need surrender. And you don't need a brand. You need the blood.

And to every believer who watches in silence—

This is your wake-up call.

If you continue to follow what he never approved, you will share in its judgment.

God is not only calling out the merchants . . . he's calling out those who keep buying.

Now is the time to break the agreement, purify your hands, and return to the altar.

REFLECT

Have I ever treated God's gifts like possessions instead of a sacred trust?

Have I fallen into the trap of measuring anointing by influence or income?

Lord, cleanse me of every trace of greed, comparison, and pride. Let me steward your presence in purity.

2 PET 2:3 KJV

"And through covetousness shall they with feigned words make merchandise of you."

CHAPTER 15: **The Hirelings Who Scattered My Sheep**

JOHN 10:12–13 KJV

"But he that is an hireling, and not the shepherd, whose own the sheep are not, seeth the wolf coming, and leaveth the sheep, and fleeth: and the wolf catcheth them, and scattereth the sheep. The hireling fleeth, because he is an hireling, and careth not for the sheep."

There is a sound of scattering in the land. It is the cry of lost sheep wandering without a shepherd—wounded, confused, and misled.

Where were the shepherds when the wolves came?

Many were behind pulpits, but their hearts were far from the sheep. They had titles, platforms, and crowds, but when the wolves came, they fled.

Why? Because they were never shepherds. They were hirelings.

A shepherd lays down his life. A hireling lays down the microphone when things get uncomfortable. A shepherd weeps over the sheep. A hireling weeps only over his own reputation.

The wolves came in the form of deception, compromise, culture, politics, and sin, and rather than fight, many pastors folded. Rather than guard the flock, they entertained it.

And the sheep were scattered.

Jesus is calling out the hirelings. Not to shame, but to expose and to call the true shepherds to rise.

If you are one who fled, repent. If you are one who's been hiding in fear, return. If you are one who knows the sheep are bleeding, pick up your staff.

This is not the hour for spiritual cowards. It is the hour for watchmen, shepherds, protectors, and fathers.

The scattering must end. The sheep must be gathered. And the wolves must be confronted.

The time for passive ministry is over. The sheep are bleeding, and heaven is roaring.

The Lord is raising up Davids again—shepherds after his own heart, who will run to the field and not from it.

No more sermons without substance. No more leaders without love. No more altars without agony.

Where are the ones who will war for the sheep? Who will rebuke the wolves? Who will carry the burden and not chase the brand?

Let them arise.

And let the wolves tremble.

The church has been flooded with voices, but starved of true shepherds. We've built stages but abandoned the pastures. We've hosted conferences, but neglected the lonely and wounded.

Some hirelings preach to be heard, not to heal. They gather crowds, not because they love the sheep, but because they love the attention. And when persecution rises, they are nowhere to be found.

God is exposing this imbalance. He is flipping the tables in the temple again, not just of merchants, but of manipulators in the pulpit. He is removing those who used the sheep to build kingdoms of self.

And still, the Shepherd's heart cries out, "Who will go? Who will love like Jesus? Who will leave the ninety-nine to find the one?"

True shepherds are not perfect, but they are present. They weep when others walk away. They correct when it's uncomfortable. They protect even when it costs them everything.

If you've been scattered, God sees you. He has not forsaken you. He is gathering his flock again, not under personalities, but under his presence.

And to every pastor still afraid to speak up: Now is not the time for silence. Now is the time to roar with truth, to stand firm in the word, and to take back the fold from the wolves.

Jesus is not coming for a scattered, broken, entertainment-addicted flock. He is coming for a bride that is *gathered*, *holy*, and *ready*.

TRUMPET CALL

Rise, watchmen. Pick up your staff.

Protect the sheep; don't entertain the wolves.

God is calling shepherds back to the field.

The remnant must cry louder than the lies.

Let every hireling repent, and every shepherd return to the wall.

JOHN 10:13 KJV

"The hireling fleeth, because he is an hireling, and careth not for the sheep."

CHAPTER 16: A Generation That Has Forgotten the Altar

JOEL 2:17 KJV

"Let the priests, the ministers of the LORD, weep between the porch and the altar, and let them say, Spare thy people, O LORD."

We are raising a generation that knows the stage but has forgotten the altar.

They know how to build a following but not how to lay down their life. They know how to perform, to post, to preach—but not how to weep between the porch and the altar.

And that's why we are powerless.

The altar was never meant to be a decorative piece at the front of the church. It was meant to be the place of death. Of surrender. Of fire.

But now? Altars are replaced with fog machines. Tears are replaced with lights. And the sacred moment of kneeling before a holy God has been traded for applause.

We will never see revival without the altar.

We will never see transformation without tears.

We will never see breakthrough without brokenness.

Let the priests weep again. Let the intercessors arise. Let the sanctuary become a house of prayer, not a platform for performance.

If you can't remember the last time you hit your knees in holy surrender, then return to the altar.

If your church doesn't know what it means to cry out, then lead them there.

The altar is where the fire falls. The altar is where joy returns. The altar is where revival begins.

Let us return, not with pride, but with ashes.

The altar is not a relic of the past; it is a requirement for the present. A church without an altar is a church without power. And a believer without an altar is a believer without oil.

We have built stages where we should have built sanctuaries. We've created brands instead of birthing breakthroughs. We've sought platforms instead of presence, and the cost is devastating.

Where are the tears of repentance? Where is the sound of travail in the sanctuary? Where are the ministers who still know how to groan in the Spirit until chains break and strongholds fall?

God is not moved by polished sermons or clever illustrations. He is moved by the heart that is broken, contrite, and trembling at his word.

ISA 66:2

"But to this man will I look, even to him that is poor and of a contrite spirit, and trembleth at my word."

That is the kind of heart that draws the fire.

We don't need more influencers; we need intercessors. We don't need more strategies; we need surrender. We don't need more fog; we need fire.

The enemy has deceived many into believing that as long as the service is excellent, God must be pleased. But heaven is not impressed with excellence; heaven responds to obedience.

If the altar is empty, the service was incomplete. If the people leave entertained but untransformed, then what was the point?

God is calling us back to the altar because he is ready to pour out his glory. But the glory always follows the sacrifice.

Romans 12:1 tells us to present our bodies as living sacrifices, not polished performances. The altar is not for comfort. It is for consecration.

It is time to tear down the idols of convenience and rebuild the altars of commitment. Time to stop rushing past the sacred moment and linger again until the Spirit falls.

Let the altar burn again, not with strange fire, but holy fire. Not for performance, but for purification. Not for applause, but for awakening.

REFLECT

- 🔥 When was the last time I truly wept before the Lord?
- 🎭 Have I traded tears for talent?
- 🏛 Is my altar dusty?

Lord, break my heart for what breaks yours. Bring me back to the altar where your fire still falls.

JOEL 2:17 KJV

"Let the priests . . . weep between the porch and the altar."

CHAPTER 17: **The Gospel That Costs Nothing, Changes Nothing**

LUKE 9:23–24 KJV

"And he said to them all, If any man will come after me, let him deny himself, and take up his cross daily, and follow me. For whosoever will save his life shall lose it: but whosoever will lose his life for my sake, the same shall save it."

There is a gospel being preached today that demands no surrender, no repentance, and no cost—and therefore, it brings no change.

It is a gospel that fills seats but empties altars. It is a gospel that entertains but never sanctifies. That blesses but never breaks. That calls you upward but never downward to your knees.

But the true gospel of Jesus Christ will cost you everything.

Jesus never promised ease. He promised a cross. He never said, "Follow your dreams." He said, "Follow me." And in that following, you will die to yourself and be raised to life.

We've raised a generation that thinks salvation is a prayer repeated once, instead of a life surrendered daily. But Christ is not a onetime transaction. He is the Lamb slain, the King enthroned, the Lord obeyed.

The gospel that saves you also changes you. If you walked an aisle but never picked up your cross, friend, go back. If you said the words but never laid down your life, go back.

This is not condemnation; it is a holy invitation. There is no such thing as a costless Christianity.

The same Jesus who died for you is calling you to die to self. And in that death . . . is life.

A gospel without cost is a gospel without Christ. What we call "modern grace," many of the early church would have called "apostasy." They didn't preach for popularity; they preached until chains were broken, until idols fell, and until cities trembled.

The apostles bled for the message. Stephen was stoned for it. Paul was imprisoned for it. John was exiled for it. And today? We filter it, water it down, and sell it as a lifestyle brand.

No more. The time has come for the real gospel to rise again.

The gospel that crucifies the flesh. The gospel that casts down pride. The gospel that doesn't just inform, but transforms.

We need a gospel that delivers the addict, not coddles the addiction. We need preaching that breaks chains, not just tickles ears.

Let the cross be preached again, not as jewelry, not as décor, but as death to the old man and resurrection to new life.

Let the altar be full again. Let the fire fall again. Let the lukewarm be shaken and the sleeping be stirred.

We don't need more influencers. We need more intercessors. We don't need more celebrity pastors. We need consecrated prophets.

If it costs you nothing, it changes nothing. But if you'll give him everything, he will give you life, and life more abundantly.

DECLARATION

I will not serve a gospel of convenience.

I will take up my cross and follow Jesus.

I will deny myself and obey his voice, even when it costs.

The gospel is not just good news; it's the power to transform.

Lord, burn away every counterfeit message. Let me live the crucified life.

LUKE 9:23 KJV

"Let him deny himself, and take up his cross daily, and follow me."

CHAPTER 18: **When Conviction Becomes Offensive**

GAL 4:16 KJV

"Am I therefore become your enemy, because I tell you the truth?"

Truth has become hate speech.

Holiness has become judgment.

Conviction has become offensive.

And anyone who dares to preach righteousness is labeled a bigot, a Pharisee, or a "problem."

We are in a time where telling the truth makes you the enemy, even in church.

We are raising a generation that is allergic to conviction, resistant to reproof, and hostile to holiness. They shout, "Don't judge me," while falling deeper into sin. They demand acceptance but reject repentance. They want to be affirmed in their rebellion, not transformed by truth.

But hear this: Truth was never meant to comfort the flesh. It was meant to crucify it.

Isa 30:10 KJV

"Which say to the seers, See not; and to the prophets,
Prophesy not unto us right things, speak unto us smooth
things, prophesy deceits."

This is the generation that wants smooth things. Pleasant sermons.
Soft words. A gospel without a cross. A Savior without surrender.

But that is not the Jesus of Scripture.

Jesus preached repentance, not relevance.
He flipped tables; he didn't cater to them.
He rebuked sin; he didn't rebrand it.

And now, when a preacher dares to say, "Repent!"; when a prophet
cries, "Come out from among them!"; when a watchman blows the
trumpet, he is called divisive, legalistic, or dangerous.
No, he is faithful.

2 Tim 4:3–4 KJV

"For the time will come when they will not endure sound
doctrine; but after their own lusts shall they heap to them-
selves teachers, having itching ears;

And they shall turn away their ears from the truth, and
shall be turned unto fables."

That time is now. The itching ears have taken over the pews, and
too many pastors have become performers instead of prophets.
They entertain goats instead of feeding sheep. They soothe the
masses but never stir the soul.

Conviction is not cruelty; it is mercy.
It is the hand of God pulling a soul from hell.
It is the fire of the Spirit exposing the cancer of sin before it
destroys.

Yes, it stings.

Yes, it offends.

But it saves.

> PROV 27:6 KJV
>
> *"Faithful are the wounds of a friend; but the kisses of an enemy are deceitful."*

Better a wound from God that heals the heart than a kiss from culture that sends you to destruction.

So what if you're called harsh?

So what if they walk away when you preach the truth?

So what if they cancel you?

You were not called to be liked; you were called to be light.

Let the world rage. Let the mockers sneer.

Let them shut their ears and cover their eyes.

But you cry aloud and spare not.

Speak the truth even if it costs you your platform.

Preach repentance even if they leave your church.

Sound the alarm even if they never say "Thank you."

Because heaven is watching.

Because Jesus is coming.

Because silence is not an option.

And if conviction offends, let it offend.

> JER 23:29 KJV
>
> *"Is not my word like as a fire? saith the Lord; and like a hammer that breaketh the rock in pieces?"*

We don't need soft sermons. We need a fire that breaks chains.

We don't need motivational speeches. We need a hammer that shatters sin.

We don't need permission to be silent; we need boldness to stand up and speak.

Let the fear of man die.

Let truth rise again.

Let conviction fall like fire.

This is not the time to back down; this is the time to burn with holy boldness.

TRUMPET CALL

Don't apologize for the truth.

Don't back down when the world resists holiness.

Don't soften what the Spirit has made sharp.

The gospel is offensive to the flesh, but it is life to the soul.

Let conviction burn again.

Let truth speak again.

Let the fear of God return to the house of God.

GAL 4:16 KJV

"Am I therefore become your enemy, because I tell you the truth?"

CHAPTER 19: **Entertained but Not Transformed**

2 Tim 4:3–4 KJV

"For the time will come when they will not endure sound doctrine; but after their own lusts shall they heap to themselves teachers, having itching ears; And they shall turn away their ears from the truth, and shall be turned unto fables."

The church today is full, but not full of power.

Many are showing up. Few are showing fruit.

We've built services that entertain but don't convict. Programs that impress but don't transform. Worship that stirs the emotions but never reaches the spirit.

And it's killing us.

This was prophesied that a day would come when people would no longer tolerate sound doctrine. Instead, they would find teachers to scratch their itching ears—preachers who would validate sin, bless rebellion, and replace repentance with motivational slogans.

That day is here.

We're not lacking sermons; we're lacking surrender. We're not short on content; we're short on conviction.

If the church looks no different than the world, what are we offering? If all we produce is a crowd, but not a cross, what have we built?

Jesus didn't come to entertain. He came to upend the world order. He didn't die to improve your mood. He died to transform your soul.

HEB 4:12 KJV

"For the word of God is quick, and powerful, and sharper than any twoedged sword, piercing even to the dividing asunder of soul and spirit, and of the joints and marrow, and is a discerner of the thoughts and intents of the heart."

The word is meant to cut us open, not coddle us. To confront sin, not comfort rebellion. When the gospel becomes entertainment, the cross becomes optional. And when the cross is optional, salvation is counterfeit.

We have worship nights that pack arenas but don't produce repentance. We have preachers with millions of followers, but no tears on the altar. We have polished productions, but little presence of God.

The Holy Spirit is not a sideshow. He is not here to make us feel goose bumps. He is here to convict, to sanctify, to burn out sin, and to empower us to live holy.

JOHN 16:8 KJV

"And when he is come, he will reprove the world of sin, and of righteousness, and of judgment."

We must return to Spirit-led gatherings where truth cuts, where hearts are pierced, where people fall on their faces, crying out for mercy. Enough with tickled ears. Let hearts burn again.

Let us return to preaching the blood. The cross. The resurrection. The judgment. The mercy. The holiness. The fire.

1 COR 2:4–5 KJV

"And my speech and my preaching was not with enticing words of man's wisdom, but in demonstration of the Spirit and of power:

That your faith should not stand in the wisdom of men, but in the power of God."

Let our gatherings be places of glory, not just gatherings.

TRUMPET CALL

The time of entertainment is over.

The church must rise in power, or she will fall in deception.

Let us strip away every performance, every shallow imitation, and every worldly distraction.

The Spirit is calling for fire-filled pulpits, repentant altars, and lives set apart.

REFLECTIVE QUESTIONS

1. Have I sought entertainment in church more than transformation?

2. Do I measure the power of a service by how it made me feel, or by how it changed my walk with Christ?

3. Am I willing to endure sound doctrine even when it cuts across my comfort?

4. What in my life needs to move from performance to true surrender?

DECLARATION

I will not settle for entertainment when my soul needs transformation.

I will not seek tickled ears when God offers a burning heart.

I return to the cross, the blood, the fire, and the power of God.

I declare that my life and my church will be places of glory, not performances.

Lord, shake everything that entertains but does not transform. Awaken my soul to your burning truth.

2 TIM 4:3–4 KJV

"They will not endure sound doctrine . . . and shall be turned unto fables."

CHAPTER 20: **You Can't Have Jesus Without Repentance**

ACTS 3:19 KJV

"Repent ye therefore, and be converted, that your sins may be blotted out, when the times of refreshing shall come from the presence of the Lord."

We love to preach Jesus as Savior. We love the mercy, the love, the forgiveness, and we should.

But we cannot skip the first word of the gospel: "Repent."

Repentance is not legalism. It is not shame. It is not condemnation. It is the open door to freedom. It is the key that unlocks refreshing. It is the cry that touches the heart of God.

There is no Jesus without repentance.

He does not enter a heart still loyal to sin. He does not bless what he came to crucify. And he does not anoint what he's trying to deliver you from.

The gospel begins with a turning, not just away from sin, but toward God.

Preach repentance again. Call for it in the streets. Cry out for it in the church. Model it in your own life. For the church that will not repent cannot lead the world to Christ.

And for every soul who thinks repentance is a onetime prayer, hear this: repentance is a lifestyle.

We must live in a posture of humility, honesty, and holiness.

God is not calling perfect people. He is calling repentant people.

And to those who turn, there is mercy still.

Many have tried to serve Jesus while clinging to sin, but the cross demands surrender. The blood of Christ is too holy to be shared with idols. We must choose: repentance or rebellion.

True repentance isn't just feeling sorry. It's fruit. It's the evidence of a changed heart, a heart that longs to obey, not just escape hell.

The church must return to the upper room posture—broken, waiting, surrendered, and seeking fire.

Revival doesn't begin with music or crowds; it begins with repentance.

Let us teach it again. Model it again. Cry out for it again.

A church that repents is a church that carries glory.

DECLARATION

[2] I will live a lifestyle of repentance.

⊥ I will not harden my heart to conviction.

♦ I will let God burn out everything that doesn't belong.

♔ I will honor the blood of Jesus by surrendering my whole life.

📖 I will preach repentance without shame and walk in holiness without apology.

ACTS 3:19 KJV

"Repent ye therefore, and be converted."

CHAPTER 21: **The Alarm Is Sounding, but Few Are Waking**

ROMANS 13:11

And that, knowing the time, that now it is high time to awake out of sleep: for now is our salvation nearer than when we believed.

The alarm is sounding.

The trumpet is blowing.

The Spirit of the living God is crying out, *"Wake up, my people!"*

And yet, in churches across the land, many roll over and hit the spiritual snooze button. Some pull the covers of comfort tighter around them. Others reach for the distraction of their phone, the next show, the next scroll, the next laugh—anything to avoid hearing the urgency of the call.

We are living in the most prophetic hour since the resurrection of Christ. Every sign he spoke of is converging before our eyes—wars and rumors of wars, nations rising against nations, famines, pestilences, earthquakes in diverse places, lawlessness abounding, and the love of many waxing cold. The fig tree is blooming. The gospel is being preached to all nations. And yet . . . the church is asleep.

THE LULLABY OF THE LAST DAYS

Why is the bride sleeping?

Because the enemy has learned how to rock her to sleep.

He has lulled her with comfort. He has distracted her with entertainment. He has intoxicated her with prosperity. He has whispered the lie that there is no urgency, that "all things continue as they were," that there's still time to live for self and give God the leftovers.

It's a satanic lullaby, and millions have fallen under its spell.

Instead of the roar of a lion, we hear the soft hum of complacency. Instead of watchmen on the wall, we see influencers on a stage. Instead of fire on the altar, there is fog on the platform. And all the while, the clock ticks closer to midnight.

THE FIRE OF THE WATCHMAN

But God is raising voices in this hour—voices that will not be silenced, voices that will not be bought, voices that will not hit snooze.

These are the watchmen who know the time. They hear the approaching hoofbeats of the King of Glory. They feel the urgency of the hour deep in their bones. They cannot be at ease while the bride sleeps and the world perishes.

The watchman's cry is not polite. It's not crafted for approval ratings. It's raw. It's loud. It's urgent.

"Wake up, O sleeper! The night is far spent! The day is at hand! Put off the works of darkness and put on the armor of light!"

If this cry irritates you, then you are probably asleep. If it stirs you, then you are closer to awakening.

THE SLEEPING BRIDE

The bride of Christ was never meant to be found napping when the bridegroom returned. Yet in Jesus' own parable of the ten virgins (Matt 25), all of them, wise and foolish alike, fell asleep.

The difference? The wise had oil in their lamps. The foolish let their oil run out.

That is where we are now. Many still have lamps; they still have the appearance of faith, but the oil of intimacy, prayer, and holiness has run dry. They have no fire when the midnight cry is heard.

Beloved, you cannot borrow oil at the last moment. You cannot wake up on the day of his return and suddenly produce a lifetime of devotion. Now is the time to fill your lamp. Now is the time to burn.

THE NEARNESS OF HIS RETURN

Jesus is not coming figuratively. He is not coming metaphorically. He is coming literally, physically, visibly, and he is coming soon.

We are not waiting for "one day in the distant future." We are racing toward the most dramatic, world-shaking event since the cross and resurrection—the return of the King of Kings.

Your salvation is nearer now than when you first believed. Your time is shorter than you think. Eternity is rushing toward us like a tidal wave, and most are playing on the shore as though the water will never rise.

Wake up.

The trumpet is not a metaphor. The trumpet of God will sound, and the dead in Christ will rise. The living who are ready will be caught up. And the rest will face the wrath of God poured out on a rebellious world.

If that does not stir you, you need to examine whether you belong to him.

THIS IS NOT THE HOUR TO SLEEP

Paul warned in 1 Thess 5:6 KJV, *"Therefore let us not sleep, as do others; but let us watch and be sober."*

This is not the hour to coast. It is not the hour to dabble in sin. It is not the hour to hide your light under a basket. This is the hour to fast, to pray, to preach, to warn, to love boldly, to forgive quickly, to live with urgency.

This is the hour to get your house in order—spiritually, relationally, financially, emotionally. This is the hour to shake off every chain and run the race to win.

Souls are hanging in the balance. The lost do not have time for you to be lukewarm. The bridegroom does not have patience for a bride who refuses to get dressed.

A HOLY WAKE-UP CALL

If you hear nothing else in this chapter, hear this: you will not get another lifetime to do what God has called you to do.

You have one life. One chance. One moment in human history to be the voice, the light, the hands, and the feet of Jesus in a dying world.

Don't waste it on trivial arguments. Don't waste it chasing the wind. Don't waste it trying to be liked by a world that hates your King.

Wake up. Rise up. Speak up.

TRUMPET CALL

- ✺ Wake up, O sleeper.

- ✺ The night is far spent. The day is at hand.

- ✺ Get your house in order. Preach the truth. Live with fire.

- ✺ Fill your lamp with oil before the cry is heard.

ROM 13:11 KJV

"Now it is high time to awake out of sleep: for now is our salvation nearer than when we believed."

CHAPTER 22: **Almost Saved Is Still Lost**

Acts 26:28 KJV

"Then Agrippa said unto Paul, Almost thou persuadest me to be a Christian."

Hell is full of people who were *almost saved*.

They heard the gospel.

They felt the conviction.

They even nodded in agreement.

But they never surrendered.

King Agrippa sat in the presence of Paul—a man burning with the fire of God, chained for the sake of Christ, declaring truth without fear. Agrippa felt the weight of eternity pressing against his heart. He was *this close* to stepping into the kingdom.

But "almost" wasn't enough.

Almost repented.

Almost believed.

Almost followed.

But *almost still ends in lost.*

The Tragedy of Almost

We've filled churches with people who are "almost" Christians.

They sing the songs, but don't know the Shepherd.

They post Bible verses, but don't obey the Bible's voice.

They raise their hands in worship, but never lay down their lives.

They admire Jesus, but they don't follow him.

They agree with the message, but never respond to it.

They've been persuaded . . . but never *converted.*

Jesus said in Matt 7:21-23 KJV,

> *"Not every one that saith unto me, Lord, Lord, shall enter
> into the kingdom of heaven; but he that doeth the will of
> my Father which is in heaven. Many will say to me in that
> day, Lord, Lord, have we not prophesied in thy name? and
> in thy name have cast out devils? and in thy name done
> many wonderful works? And then will I profess unto them,
> I never knew you: depart from me, ye that work iniquity."*

Friend, you can know *about* him and still not truly know him.

You can be near the kingdom and still be outside its gates.

You can be "almost" there and still hear him say, "I never knew you."

The Deception of Delay

"Almost" is the word of the procrastinator.

"I'll repent tomorrow."

"I'll surrender when I'm older."

"I'll follow him after I get through this season."

But Prov 27:1 KJV warns,

> *"Boast not thyself of to morrow; for thou knowest not what a day may bring forth."*

Hell is filled with people who *planned* to get saved one day.

They intended to pray, but never did.

They intended to change, but the change never came.

Almost saved is still lost.

The rich young ruler in Mark 10:17–22 came running to Jesus. He wanted eternal life. He knew the commandments. He looked the part. But when Jesus told him to sell all, give to the poor, and follow him, *he walked away sorrowful*. Why? Because he was almost willing, but not willing enough.

The Danger of Comfort

Many will never cross the line from "almost" to "all" because comfort is their god.

They fear losing friends.

They fear being mocked.

They fear the cost of obedience more than they fear the cost of disobedience.

But Jesus made it plain in Luke 14:27 KJV,

"And whosoever doth not bear his cross, and come after me, cannot be my disciple."

He did not say, "Try me for a season."

He did not say, "Add me to your life."

He said, "Follow me, and die to yourself daily."

Almost salvation preaches a cross-less Christ.

True salvation bows at the foot of the cross and leaves the old life buried there.

From Almost to All

The gospel demands decision.

There is no neutral ground.

In 2 Cor 6:2 KJV, it says,

> *"Behold, now is the accepted time; behold, now is the day of salvation."*

If you feel him calling—*answer.*

If you hear the knock—*open.*

If you know the truth—*obey.*

Agrippa heard the truth and walked away unchanged. Let his name be a warning.

Don't sit under conviction and do nothing. Don't be stirred but not moved. Don't get "close" to the kingdom and then walk away.

Almost won't save you. Only all will.

TRUMPET CALL

- ↝ Almost is not enough—give him everything.
- ↝ Do not delay. Tomorrow is not promised.
- ↝ Lay down every idol, every excuse, every sin.
- ↝ Step fully into the kingdom—today.

DECLARATION

- † I refuse to be almost. I give Jesus my all.
- ◖ I will not delay repentance another day.
- ⓘ I will surrender every corner of my heart to him.
- ♛ I belong fully to the King—now and forever.

Lord, I don't want to be almost. I want to be fully yours.

ACTS 26:28 KJV

"Almost thou persuadest me to be a Christian."

CHAPTER 23: **The Time Is Now**

2 COR 6:2 KJV

"For he saith, I have heard thee in a time accepted, and in the day of salvation have I succoured thee: behold, now is the accepted time; behold, now is the day of salvation."

This is it.

This is the moment, not next week, not next year, not when you've "got it all together."

Now.

Now is the time to repent. Now is the time to return. Now is the time to rise, to obey, to follow, to burn.

This is the final call.

God is no longer winking at sin. He is shaking everything that can be shaken. He is tearing down idols. He is exposing what's been hidden. He is waking up his remnant.

Because he loves us too much to let us sleep through eternity.

The day of salvation is not on your calendar. It is not penciled in for a better time. It is not waiting for your convenience.

It is right now.

For the backslider—come home.

For the lukewarm—get in or get out.

For the lost—there's still mercy.

For the called—rise and run.

For the church—repent and burn again.

This isn't hype. It's holy urgency.

The door is still open, but it will not stay open forever.

The prophets warned of a day when men would harden their hearts beyond repair. Jesus himself told of the five wise and five foolish virgins—those who were ready, and those who thought they had more time. The door was shut to the foolish, not because God delighted in it, but because the hour had come and gone.

MATT 25:13 KJV

"Watch therefore, for ye know neither the day nor the hour wherein the Son of man cometh."

Every heartbeat is borrowed mercy. Every sunrise is a gift to repent. Every sermon you hear, every warning you receive, is an act of divine love pleading with you, "Don't wait. Come now."

HEB 3:15 KJV

"While it is said, To day if ye will hear his voice, harden not your hearts, as in the provocation."

The longer you wait, the harder it becomes. Sin numbs the soul. Delay deafens the ears. And before you know it, the conviction you once felt will fade, not because God has stopped speaking, but because you have stopped listening.

Believer, hear me: There is no revival without urgency. There is no awakening without movement. The Spirit is calling for watchmen to cry aloud, for intercessors to weep between the porch and the altar, for evangelists to run with the gospel like men on fire.

We are not promised another year, another month, or another day.

JAS 4:14 KJV

"Whereas ye know not what shall be on the morrow. For what is your life? It is even a vapour, that appeareth for a little time, and then vanisheth away."

So why do we live as though tomorrow is guaranteed? Why do we postpone obedience when eternity hangs in the balance?

If the Spirit has been nudging you to forgive, do it now.
If he's been calling you to repentance, do it now.
If he's been stirring you to preach, to serve, to give, to go, do it now.

Postponed obedience is present disobedience.

We have had enough delay. The King is at the door. His reward is in his hand. The trumpet is at his lips.

REV 22:12 KJV

"And, behold, I come quickly; and my reward is with me, to give every man according as his work shall be."

Will he find you faithful? Will he find you burning? Or will he find you distracted, drowsy, and entangled in the cares of life?

LUKE 21:34 KJV

"And take heed to yourselves, lest at any time your hearts be overcharged with surfeiting, and drunkenness, and cares of this life, and so that day come upon you unawares."

Shake off the slumber. Tear down the idols. Lift up your head, for your redemption is drawing near.

DECLARATION

🔥 I will not wait another moment.

🕊 I will answer the call of the Spirit.

🔒 I will not delay what God demands now.

⏳ I will live with urgency, purity, and fire.

This is not just another day. This is the day of salvation.

2 COR 6:2 KJV

"Behold, now is the accepted time; behold, now is the day of salvation."

CHAPTER 24: **When Casual Faith Became a Curse**

REV 3:15–16 KJV

"I know thy works, that thou art neither cold nor hot: I would thou wert cold or hot. So then because thou art lukewarm, and neither cold nor hot, I will spue thee out of my mouth."

Casual faith is killing the church.

Once, following Jesus meant laying down your life. Now, in many places, it means fitting him in when it's convenient.

Once, discipleship meant sacrifice. Now, it often means attendance without transformation.

We have built a culture that treats Christ as an accessory, not the King. A comfort, not a consuming fire.

Lukewarm living is more dangerous than outright rejection. At least the cold know they are lost. The lukewarm think they are fine, and that deception is deadly.

When casual faith takes root, sin is excused, holiness is optional, and the Great Commission is replaced with personal comfort. The church loses her roar, her witness, and her fire.

The danger? The longer we remain lukewarm, the more comfortable we become with a powerless Christianity, and the easier it is for Satan to keep us asleep.

We must return to the Jesus who said, "Take up your cross and follow me." We must again preach a gospel that costs everything but gives more than we could ever imagine.

Casual faith is not harmless; it's a curse. And unless it is repented of, it will damn more souls than open rebellion.

This is not a time for halfhearted faith. This is the hour for radical obedience, burning love, and unwavering boldness.

The bridegroom is coming. And he is not returning for a lukewarm bride.

TRUMPET CALL

- ↩ Reject casual Christianity.

- ↩ Let your love for Christ consume you.

- ↩ Trade comfort for commitment—convenience for covenant.

- ↩ Live so fully for Jesus that the world cannot mistake your allegiance.

Let the fire fall again. Let the lukewarm be set ablaze.

CHAPTER 25: **When the King Comes**

MATT 24:44 KJV

"Therefore be ye also ready: for in such an hour as ye think not the Son of man cometh."

The King is coming.

Not as the Lamb to be slain. Not in weakness. Not in the humility of Bethlehem's manger. He is coming as the Lion of Judah—the conquering King, the Judge of the nations, the one whose eyes are a flame of fire and whose voice shakes the heavens and the earth.

And yet, many in the church live as though his return is a distant myth, not an imminent reality.

We speak of him as if he were far off, but the word says he stands at the door. We plan our lives as if the world will go on forever, but the Bible warns that in an hour we do not expect, he will split the skies.

Every prophecy about his first coming was fulfilled with precision. Every prophecy about his second coming will be fulfilled just as surely. And we are the generation watching the stage being set before our eyes.

But here is the question: Are we ready?

We prepare for weddings, for careers, and for vacations, but are we prepared to meet the King? Are our garments white, or are they stained with compromise? Are our lamps full of oil, or have we let them burn out?

When the King comes, there will be no time to get ready. You will either be ready or you will not.

The wise will be watching, their eyes fixed on the skies, their hearts fixed on his word, their lives surrendered to his will. The foolish will be distracted, asleep, busy with the temporary while ignoring the eternal.

And on that day, no excuse will stand.

Not "I was busy."
Not "I didn't think it would be now."
Not "I meant to get right later."

Later will be gone. The door will be shut. And the King will separate the sheep from the goats, the wheat from the tares, the faithful from the faithless.

This is why the Spirit cries, "Prepare the way of the Lord!" The trumpet call is not for a distant day; it is for this day. For now. For you.

When the King comes, the nations will mourn. Kings and rulers will tremble. The proud will be brought low, and the humble exalted. Every knee will bow. Every tongue will confess that Jesus Christ is Lord, willingly or unwillingly.

If you belong to him, this is not a day to dread; it is the day you have longed for. The day faith becomes sight. The day tears are wiped away. The day evil is crushed forever.

But if your heart is far from him, if you are lukewarm, if you have played the part of a Christian but never surrendered, this will be the most terrifying day of your existence.

Beloved, hear me: You do not have to face that day in fear. The blood of Jesus is still enough. Repent now. Return now. Live ready now.

Because when the King comes . . . it will be too late to decide.

REFLECT

- If he came today, would I be found faithful?
- Have I let compromise creep into my walk?
- Am I watching with expectation or sleeping in distraction?

DECLARATION

I will live ready.

I will not be caught unaware.

My lamp will be full, my garments clean, my heart burning.

When the King comes, I will be found watching.

MATT 24:44 KJV

"Therefore be ye also ready: for in such an hour as ye think not the Son of man cometh."

TRUMPET CALL

- Live every day as if this were the day of his return.
- Keep your lamp full of oil—the oil of intimacy with him.
- Refuse the distractions that dull your watchfulness.
- Let the cry of your heart be, "Even so, come, Lord Jesus."

CHAPTER 26: **Heaven Weeps for the Sleeping Bride**

Eph 5:14 KJV

"Wherefore he saith, Awake thou that sleepest, and arise from the dead, and Christ shall give thee light."

Heaven is not silent about the condition of the church. The hosts of glory look upon the bride of Christ, chosen, redeemed, called to shine, and weep when they see her slumbering in the shadow of her calling.

The angels who witnessed the empty tomb, who beheld the risen Lord, who watched the fire fall at Pentecost—those same messengers now see a church content with comfort, lulled by distraction, and rocked into a spiritual coma by the lullabies of the world. The bride, who was meant to burn with holy fire, lies wrapped in blankets of complacency.

The devil knows that a sleeping church is a silent church. He fears the praying saint, the fasting intercessor, the bold witness who carries the gospel like a burning torch. So he rocks the bride to sleep with the rhythm of entertainment, the hum of busyness, and the soft whisper of "You have time."

But heaven knows time is nearly gone.

If the church would wake up—truly wake up—the ripple would shake nations. Entire towns would repent in a day. Families would be restored. Corruption would crumble. Demons would flee. Revival would roar through streets and cities. Hell's gates would tremble under the footsteps of a mobilized bride.

The sorrow of heaven is not hopelessness; it is longing. Longing for the bride to remember her first love. Longing for her to rise, put on her wedding garments, and trim her lamp for the bridegroom's arrival.

We must understand: sleep is not neutral. While we slumber, the enemy sows tares. While we doze, the lost die without Christ. While we nap, deception spreads. This is why heaven weeps: because the potential of the church is being squandered in the haze of spiritual drowsiness.

The voice of the Spirit is crying, "Wake up, O sleeper! Rise from the dead, and Christ will shine on you." This is not a suggestion; it is a rescue call. The night is far spent. The day is at hand.

We must shake off the slumber, cast off the works of darkness, and clothe ourselves with the armor of light. We must return to the altar until prayer once again feels like breath in our lungs. We must hunger for the word until it is sweeter than honey and more necessary than bread.

Heaven does not weep forever. A day is coming when the bride will be ready, dressed in white, her lamp burning bright. But whether you are part of that company depends on the choice you make now.

Will you sleep? Or will you rise?

Let the cry of heaven reach your spirit. Let it shake you. Let it move you from complacency to consecration.

The bridegroom is coming. And he is worthy of a bride who is wide awake.

TRUMPET CALL

- Wake up, O bride of Christ!
- Cast off the blankets of complacency.
- Trim your lamp and keep it burning.
- Live as though the bridegroom were coming tonight.

DECLARATION

- I will not be found sleeping when my Lord returns.
- I will seek him with urgency and passion.
- I will live as a prepared bride, ready for my King.

CHAPTER 27: **The Work of the Awake Bride**

REV 19:7 KJV

"Let us be glad and rejoice, and give honour to him: for the marriage of the Lamb is come, and his wife hath made herself ready."

The bridegroom is coming. Not in a distant, far-off generation, but soon. The bride of Christ cannot afford to be drowsy, distracted, or divided.

An awake bride is a dangerous bride—dangerous to hell, deadly to compromise, and dazzling in holiness. She is not merely waiting for the sound of the trumpet; she is preparing for it.

The question is: If we claim to be awake, what should we be doing until he comes?

Stay Pure for the Bridegroom

2 COR 11:2 KJV

"For I am jealous over you with godly jealousy: for I have espoused you to one husband, that I may present you as a chaste virgin to Christ."

The awake bride keeps her heart, mind, and body pure. She guards her eyes from lust, her ears from lies, and her lips from gossip. She refuses to flirt with the world's system.

Purity is not just avoiding sin; it's being set apart for one Person. Like a faithful bride who refuses any other suitor, she lives to please the bridegroom alone.

In this hour, purity will cost you friends, opportunities, and invitations. But it will gain you something far greater—the smile of the one you love.

Keep the Lamp Burning

MATT 25:4 KJV

"But the wise took oil in their vessels with their lamps."

The awake bride is a carrier of God's fire. She doesn't depend on yesterday's oil. She keeps going back to the secret place, filling up on the presence of the Holy Spirit.

This means daily worship, prayer, fasting, and time in the word. Not out of religious duty, but because she refuses to run dry.

When the midnight cry comes, only those with burning lamps will be ready to meet the bridegroom. Oil cannot be borrowed at the last minute. Keep yours full now.

Watch and Pray

LUKE 21:36 KJV

"Watch ye therefore, and pray always, that ye may be accounted worthy to escape all these things."

An awake bride is not caught off guard. She has eyes to see the signs of the times and a heart that stays in tune with heaven.

Prayer keeps her sober. Watching keeps her ready. The world may mock her for being "too intense," but she knows the hour is late.

This is not the time for casual, sleepy prayers. It is the time for midnight intercession—for standing in the gap for the lost, for nations, for revival.

Make Herself Ready

REV 19:7 KJV

"And his wife hath made herself ready."

Readiness is not automatic; it is intentional. The awake bride examines her life under the light of the Holy Spirit, allowing him to cleanse what doesn't belong.

She forgives quickly. She obeys immediately. She lives uncluttered by the weight of bitterness or the chains of worldliness.

Every day she asks, "If he came right now, would I be ready to look him in the eyes?"

Call Others to the Wedding

MATT 22:9 KJV

"Go ye therefore into the highways, and as many as ye shall find, bid to the marriage."

An awake bride is not content to go to the wedding feast alone. She becomes a herald—an evangelist, a soul-winner, a messenger of mercy.

She warns the complacent, reaches for the lost, and loves the unlovable. Her heart beats with the heartbeat of the bridegroom: "Go out quickly and bring them in."

She knows the invitation won't always be open. She shares it while there is still time.

Refuse Spiritual Slumber

Rom 13:11 KJV

"It is high time to awake out of sleep."

The awake bride fights against apathy like a soldier in battle. She recognizes when comfort is lulling her to sleep and shakes it off.

She refuses the sedation of entertainment, gossip, greed, or distraction. She knows the devil's lullabies are meant to keep her ineffective.

Every morning, she rises with this resolve: "Today I will not sleep through my calling."

Serve the Bridegroom Faithfully Until He Comes

Matt 24:46 KJV

"Blessed is that servant, whom his lord when he cometh shall find so doing."

The awake bride works the harvest until the last second. She doesn't sit on the porch waiting for the wedding day; she is in the fields, reaping souls, serving others, and shining his light.

She knows the bridegroom will not ask, "Were you comfortable?," but, "Were you faithful?"

TRUMPET CALL

- ᴏᴩ Keep your garments spotless—live in holiness.

- ᴏᴩ Stay filled with the oil of the Spirit—keep your flame bright.

- ᴏᴩ Watch and pray—don't be caught unaware.

- ᴏᴩ Call others to the feast—the door will soon shut.

- ᴏᴩ Refuse to sleep—stay alert and active.

- ᴏᴩ Serve faithfully—until you see him face-to-face.

DECLARATION

I am the bride of Christ, awake and ready.

I will live pure, holy, and burning for him.

I will call others to the wedding feast.

I will not be found sleeping, but serving.

CHAPTER 28: The Cost of Silence

Ezekiel 33:7–8 KJV

"So thou, O son of man, I have set thee a watchman unto the house of Israel; therefore thou shalt hear the word at my mouth, and warn them from me. When I say unto the wicked, O wicked man, thou shalt surely die; if thou dost not speak to warn the wicked from his way, that wicked man shall die in his iniquity; but his blood will I require at thine hand."

There is a cost to silence. Not just in lost opportunities. Not just in broken relationships. But in souls.

In this late hour, God has called his people to be watchmen—to stand on the wall, see the danger coming, and sound the alarm. But too many have climbed down from the wall to keep their hands clean and their reputations safe.

We have traded the boldness of the apostles for the politeness of the age. We have muted the warnings of the word because we fear offending more than we fear God. And heaven is grieved.

Silence has a price, and it is far too high.

1. Silence Enables Sin

When the church is silent, sin flourishes unchecked. Evil needs no encouragement—only the absence of resistance. Darkness does not advance because it is stronger than the light, but because the light refuses to shine.

When pulpits refuse to preach against adultery, fornication, pride, greed, and idolatry, those sins take root and grow like weeds in the garden of God. When Christians refuse to speak up about injustice, corruption, and false teaching, they create a vacuum where lies can breathe freely.

God told Ezekiel that if we see the wicked in their way and say nothing, we are not innocent but are responsible. Their blood will be required at our hands.

2. Silence Misrepresents the Gospel

A silent church is a false witness. We cannot claim to follow the one who is called "the Truth" and then hide that truth to maintain peace.

Jesus was not crucified because he blended in. He was crucified because he declared the kingdom, called out hypocrisy, confronted sin, and told men to repent.

When we soften the gospel to avoid confrontation, we preach another gospel—one without a cross, without a cost, without a Savior worth dying for.

A gospel without confrontation is a gospel without conversion.

3. Silence Forfeits Souls

This is not theory; it's eternity. Every day, people around us are stepping into forever—some into the joy of the Lord, many into the torment of hell. And for too many, the last Christian they spoke to never once mentioned salvation.

We are not called to merely "live a good example" in front of people. The apostles did not die for being good neighbors. They died because they opened their mouths and preached Jesus as the only way to God.

When we are silent, people do not automatically "figure it out." They die without hearing the truth that could have saved them. And make no mistake, God will ask why we stayed silent.

4. Silence Brings Judgment on the Silent

The fear of man is a snare, but the fear of God is the beginning of wisdom. When God calls his people to speak and they refuse, it is not only the sinner who faces judgment; the messenger is also held accountable.

Ezekiel's warning was clear: If you fail to sound the alarm, their blood is on your hands. This is not to condemn you; it is to awaken you. The Judge of all the earth is watching. The time for excuses is over.

5. It's Time to Break the Silence

This is not the moment to retreat. This is the moment to roar.

—Speak truth at your dinner table.
—Speak truth in your workplace.
—Speak truth on the street.
—Speak truth in your pulpit.

Don't wait for a perfect moment—the moment is now. Don't wait until you feel brave—courage comes when you step out.

The Spirit of God is raising up voices in this hour—prophetic voices, street preachers, evangelists, everyday believers who will not be muzzled by culture or fear.

The world is shouting lies at full volume. It's time for the church to match and surpass its volume with the truth of the gospel.

TRUMPET CALL

- ↩ Watchman, take your place on the wall.

- ↩ The hour is late, and the danger is near.

- ↩ Lift up your voice like a trumpet—warn, plead, preach, and call to repentance.

If you stay silent, hell will not. If you delay, darkness will not. The cost of silence is too high. Speak now—before it's too late.

Ezek 33:8 KJV

"Their blood will I require at thine hand."

A Call to Repentance

Rom 13:11 KJV

"And that, knowing the time, that now it is high time to awake out of sleep: for now is our salvation nearer than when we believed."

The Spirit of the Lord is speaking with urgency to this generation: The time is now. Not tomorrow. Not next Sunday.

Not when life slows down or the kids are grown. Now.

We are living in the most dangerous hour for the human soul, not because of wars, or pandemics, or political chaos, but because of the great deception sweeping through the earth: that you can be close to God without repentance.

Repentance Is Not an Option

Repentance is not a suggestion for the "super spiritual." It is not a dusty word from an outdated religious era.

Repentance is the very first step into the kingdom of God. It is the doorway through which every saint has entered.

John the baptist prepared the way for Jesus with one cry: "Repent."

Jesus began his public ministry with one cry: "Repent."

Peter preached at Pentecost with one cry: "Repent."

Heaven's message has not changed, but our pulpits have.

We have replaced turning from sin with tolerating sin. We've replaced conviction with compliments.

We've swapped the fire of the altar for the fog machine of the stage.

But the word of God still thunders:

ACTS 3:19 KJV

"Repent ye therefore, and be converted, that your sins may be blotted out."

Repentance Is More Than Regret

Saying "I'm sorry" is not repentance. Feeling bad is not repentance. Repentance is turning away from sin, toward God.

It is a decisive break from the darkness that once enslaved you.

It is not just about avoiding bad behavior; it is about surrendering lordship.

It is about removing yourself from the throne of your life and letting Jesus reign.

Real repentance doesn't just remove sin; it replaces it with holiness. It doesn't just say "no" to the devil; it says "yes" to the will of God.

Why God Commands It Now

God is shaking the nations. He is uncovering the hidden. He is dismantling false securities.

Why? Because he loves you too much to let you sleep your way into hell.

We are not promised tomorrow. We are not promised another altar call. We are not promised another breath.

Some reading this will stand before God far sooner than you think. And when that moment comes, your bank account, your résumé, your popularity—none of it will matter. The only question will be:

Did you repent and believe the gospel?

What Repentance Produces

When you truly repent:

- —your sins are blotted out (Acts 3:19), not covered, not hidden, but erased.
- —times of refreshing come—the Holy Spirit restores joy, peace, and life to your soul.
- —your desires change—you no longer crave the chains that once bound you.
- —heaven rejoices—angels throw a celebration when one sinner repents (Luke 15:10).

This is why the devil hates repentance—it is the point at which he loses his claim over you.

The Tragedy of Delay

Hell is filled with people who intended to repent "later." They were "almost persuaded" like King Agrippa, but not converted.

They thought they had time. They thought conviction would come again. But the call grew quieter until it was gone.

If you feel the Spirit stirring you now, this is mercy.

Don't harden your heart. Don't wait for a "better" time. There will never be a better time than the moment God is calling you.

CHAPTER 29: The Final Call—A Prayer of Repentance

Joel 2:12–13 KJV

"Therefore also now, saith the LORD, turn ye even to me with all your heart, and with fasting, and with weeping, and with mourning: And rend your heart, and not your garments, and turn unto the LORD your God: for he is gracious and merciful, slow to anger, and of great kindness, and repenteth him of the evil."

The Spirit of God is calling.

Not for tomorrow. Not for when life feels more convenient. Not when you "get things straightened out."

This is the final call, not just for the lost, but for the lukewarm, the backslider, and the churchgoer who has never truly surrendered.

Heaven is pleading. Hell is raging. Eternity is waiting.

God is not asking for a portion of your life. He is demanding all of it.

Every secret sin. Every hidden idol. Every private compromise. Lay it down.

We are not promised another day. The door of mercy is still open, but it will not remain open forever.

Acts 17:30 KJV says, *"And the times of this ignorance God winked at; but now commandeth all men every where to repent."*

Repentance is not simply saying, "I'm sorry." It is a holy turning. A renouncing of the old life and a surrender to Jesus as Lord.

A Step-by-Step Prayer of Repentance

Father, I come to you in the name of Jesus Christ. I acknowledge that I have sinned against you. I confess my sins before you now— every thought, word, and action that has dishonored you.

I believe that Jesus Christ is the Son of God, that he died for my sins, and that he rose again on the third day. I believe his blood is the only thing that can wash me clean.

Right now, I turn away from my sins. I lay down my pride, my rebellion, my self-will. I renounce every work of darkness. I break agreement with every lie, addiction, or chain that has held me.

Lord Jesus, I invite you into my heart as my Lord and Savior. Rule and reign over my life. Fill me with the Holy Spirit. Empower me to live for you all the days of my life.

From this moment on, I am yours completely and forever. I will follow you, obey you, and love you with all my heart, soul, mind, and strength.

Amen.

TRUMPET CALL

- ✌ Do not delay.

- ✌ Live holy. Live ready. Live burning.

- ✌ Let the world see Christ in you.

REVELATION 3:19 KJV

"As many as I love, I rebuke and chasten: be zealous therefore, and repent."

This is not just a prayer; it is the beginning of a new life. Rise now and walk in it.

ROMANS 13:11 KJV

"And that, knowing the time, that now it is high time to awake out of sleep: for now is our salvation nearer than when we believed."